NEVER GIVE UP

 FriesenPress

Suite 300 - 990 Fort St
Victoria, BC, V8V 3K2
Canada

www.friesenpress.com

ISBN
978-1-5255-6370-6 (Hardcover)
978-1-5255-6371-3 (Paperback)
978-1-5255-6372-0 (eBook)

1. SELF-HELP, PERSONAL GROWTH, HAPPINESS

Distributed to the trade by The Ingram Book Company

NEVER GIVE UP

12 WAYS TO HAVE AN OUTSTANDING LIFE

TOM SHINDRUK

Table of Contents

YOUR GOALS DON'T START IN YOUR HEAD,
THEY START IN YOUR HEART

**Twelve Ways to Have
an Extraordinary Life**

Introduction

Every human being who has ever lived, or who will live, wants to have a good life. All want to be successful, wealthy, wise, and well liked. We can have all of this, and more, if we are willing to do something about making changes in our lives if we are not satisfied with what we have. What do we believe that success means? It is different with different people. Some think that being rich, having a lot of money, is success. Some want to show others how smart they are, that they have great wisdom. Everyone wants to be popular, well liked, and yet many don't work at building relationships that are lasting. Everyone who I have ever met wishes they would win the lottery, but very few do. Everyone wants to be loved, but many don't find the love that they crave. How many lack confidence? How many don't like the way they look, their body shape, their hair, their nose or ears; they're just not happy with their appearance. How many resort to plastic surgery, implants, removal of warts and so-called beauty marks and then find out later that they have major health issues or they don't like the results of these changes to their bodies or faces?

Most of us, especially when we are young, really don't think about what we have done in the past that could have serious results later in life. Smoking starts when we are young, and many are refusing to believe that use of tobacco products causes cancer. Overeating and obesity is the cause of many health issues, such as heart problems, diabetes, stroke, and so many other medical issues too numerous to mention. What about psychological affects when we are overweight: clothes don't fit and we are unable to participate in various sports or other activities. How important is appearance? How do we feel about ourselves? If we don't like ourselves, how can we expect others to like us? There are challenges that we face from the time we are young until we die.

What Is Happiness?

My life has been an exciting journey, with many challenges and trials and tribulations, but somehow it all turned out well. Today, at 84 years old, my life has never been better. How did this evolve from my early memories of growing up on a small mixed farm in Manitoba? My parents were the first generation of immigrants from the Ukraine and Poland.—born before the First World War. They married and raised their children during the Great Depression. The imprint that all the people in our lives leave on us is the way we turn out. If we had a positive upbringing, then we are probably quite positive and enjoy a good life. On the other hand, if our childhood was difficult, with negativity and violence, then our lives will possibly be one with serious challenges that many cannot handle and we live with discouragements and depression. There are many individuals in my life who have had a most positive imprint on my life, some from my childhood and then throughout my varied work career. We are not alone in this world, and, during our time here on earth, it would make sense to get along with others and to create a life where we are happy and successful. How we do that will depend entirely on what happened when we were very young. I was very lucky, my parents were wonderful, loving, and encouraged us to strive to be better. I have two brothers: Bob is older and Lloyd is younger than I; we had, and still have, a great relationship. We meet somewhere every year for a few days to reminisce and spend time with each other. The love we have for each other shows and sends a message to others that it is important to get along well with your family members. My brothers are retired like me, but are still active by volunteering and doing things for others.

Who helped us in our careers, did we have mentors, and are we mentors to others as we gain experience and knowledge? How do we picture and react to the events, both good and bad, in our lifetime? Events and people in our lives form our personality and character, and also how we perceive these events. If we approach each event, difficult or otherwise, with the right attitude and have help from others, we mostly will enjoy the journey. Life should be a joy and not a struggle. It is all up to us and what are our perceptions of what we face and then how we react and eventually become a person that enjoys life as it is meant to be.

I want to share some of my experiences and knowledge so that you, too, can have a full life, one filled with happiness, health, wealth, and success. My life since my early childhood has been one with good and challenging times. Much of our lives are like that, hopefully just living day to day, working, sleeping, eating, and doing things in our leisure time. Then we also experience challenges. I was married at age twenty, to a beautiful, kind, intelligent, and elegant woman. She also turned out to be a wonderful wife, a fantastic mother, an excellent housekeeper, and an unbelievable cook. Some of my experiences were challenging during our early days of marriage. Of course, some were difficult at first: buying our first home, getting a better job, the birth of our two sons. And then we were transferred from Winnipeg to Toronto. This was our huge upheaval, leaving both my family and my wife's family behind, 1,500 miles away, moving to a strange city with two little boys and also a new set of fellow workers, new territory, and more obligations and opportunities. The first challenge was that the money that I was supposed to get with the move was less than expected, and I had to take a part-time job for a period of time in order to, first, qualify for a mortgage, and then pay it. I worked at my regular job as a merchandiser, covering the province of Ontario, and worked part time at a grocery store filling shelves at night. This was done for almost a year, until I was promoted to

Supervisor of Merchandising for Canada. This gave me a salary increase, and now I didn't need the part-time work. And, owing to increased travel across the country, I was not able to do the grocery job anymore. I never gave up.

As a result of the supervisory position, I was also used in the United States as a trainer of new hires, and was asked to be the trouble-shooter, now called dispute resolution. This was mostly very stressful, as I was required to solve issues that could affect people's lives. My 18 years in the citrus business were absolutely wonderful, full of learning opportunities and networking. Plus, it enabled me to visit almost all of the United States and Canada. I am considered an expert in the citrus and fresh produce industry.

After moving to Calgary in the early 1970s, running the local office was a great, rewarding experience, and the biggest bonus was we had a new addition to our family—a beautiful daughter. Now we had two amazing sons and a princess, and our family was complete.

In the mid-1970s, owing to differences in career paths, I resigned from my long-time job and we bought a hotel with a partner in Drumheller. This was huge change in the type of work that I was accustomed to doing, but our partnership was good and we turned a poorly run business into a success. In fact, we were offered a price for the business that was easy to accept. Shortly after the hotel was sold, my partner died and our plans for another hotel were shelved.

This was stressful, losing a partner and a friend. We moved back to Calgary and I found employment as a realtor. After a couple of years, I did not get satisfaction from this type of work and was hired to improve the sales of the largest fresh potato packing company in Alberta. Again, I had stress in the work I undertook but I succeeded, and when my contract was up, I went to work as the sales manager of a large food service distributor.

Managing a staff of 46 outside and inside salespeople was an amazing experience, with lots of stress and a great deal of accomplishment. Several other opportunities were taken and eventually the real challenges in our lives started to come. In 1982, our oldest son was stricken with a serious illness: a virus attacked his brain and he was prone to grand mal seizures. His marriage fell apart, his business was sold, and, for 27 years, he was seriously affected. He was unable to work or to have a normal life. But we all pulled together; our family became closer and stronger.

In 1999, I was suddenly shoved into the world of cancer, with major surgery. Full recovery was possible and life returned to normal. In 2001, cancer hit me again, this time in the prostate. Treatment was applied, hormonal, and all came out well. Then, in 2004, the prostate cancer came back, and this time we elected to go with radiation treatment. In November and December of 2004, I received 38 treatments at the Foothills Tom Baker Cancer Hospital. I survived and recovered, and life returned to what we expected. I never gave up.

In 2008, our oldest son passed away peacefully in his sleep at the age of 52. Our hearts broke—all of us—our family was devastated, but we again bonded, pulled together, supported each other, and came through. We never gave up.

In 2011, I suddenly started to hemorrhage and ended up in the Foothills Hospital and almost died. I was given nine units of blood in three days. I survived and was released after a week. In 2011, I was diagnosed with type 2 diabetes. However, with the loving support of my wife and my children and friends, I am healthy and happy.

Challenges will be with us throughout our lives. It's not the challenges that will devastate us; it's how we handle the challenges that will enable us to overcome and grow. Just never give up. Be brave!

SKILLS REQUIRED FOR SUCCESS IN LIFE

» Be a powerful communicator.
» Create meaningful personal and business goals to drive you forward.
» Develop mental toughness and a strong positive attitude.
» Be a master networker.
» Take control of important situations—learn how to stay in charge.
» Be a master negotiator.
» Eliminate self-doubt—have a healthy prosperity consciousness.
» Be a good money manager.
» Take time off, including several vacations each year.
» Be excellent at building important relationships.
» Develop the ability to see the future with clarity.
» Focus on priorities—work smarter, delegate unnecessary tasks, use technology.

Chapter 1
TAKE A CHANCE—
BE BRAVE

*I look to the future, because that's where
I'm going to spend the rest of my life.* —George Burns (at age 87)

*No pessimist ever discovered the secrets of the stars, or sailed to an
uncharted island, or opened a new heaven to the human spirit.*
—Helen Keller

An essential aspect of creativity is not being afraid to fail.
—Edwin Rand

*Be not afraid. Believe that life is worth living,
and your belief will help create the fact.* —William James

*The greatest mistake anyone can make is
to be afraid of making one.* —Elbert Hubbard

*Don't be afraid to go out on the limb,
that's where the fruit is.* —Arthur F. Lenhan

How brave were our grandparents? Mine must have been
extremely brave. They immigrated to Canada from the Ukraine
in 1901. Their living conditions back in the late 1800s must have

been horrific. From the stories my grandmother told me, it was bad. There was no middle class, only the very rich and the very poor, and they were in the very poor category, with no promise of a better future. So, they sold everything and came to Canada. Two adults with four children leaving their home never to return, moving to an unknown land and an uncertain future, but they didn't give up, they moved on.

They were leaving a part of Ukraine that had a moderate climate, where they grew fruits and nuts and temperatures hardly ever went to a serious below zero. The move to Canada was to Manitoba, with no roads, no homes, not even the barest of comforts that they had enjoyed in the old country. Many others, too, immigrated to Canada, and quite a few from their village came at the same time and settled in that area of Manitoba and perhaps that made them feel a bit safer. But still, it took a lot of bravery to make the decision to leave what was probably fairly comfortable, owning a house and some land, even though it was a small plot, with a promise of 160-acre homestead in a strange and foreign land.

They began a new life without any assurance of success. The unknown must have been scary, especially as they did not read or write in any language, neither English nor Ukrainian, but with faith, they came to Canada, and I am so glad they did; what a wonderful country they built.

I recall growing up on the farm in Manitoba. Born in the Great Depression, I know that even though my parents were poor, we were never hungry, cold, or abused. We lived on the same farm, my grandfather's homestead, in the beautiful rolling hills south of Riding Mountain National Park, with our grandparents, and everyone worked together. I am certain that the difficulties experienced during those trying times were enormous, but my parents had to be brave and somehow survived and brought up their children to be survivors, too. Their bravery and struggles must

TOM SHINDRUK

have been monumental. My mother told us that many times all they had was about five dollars to last them for the whole winter. Luckily, my dad was a violinist and played at dances and weddings and would bring home two or three dollars for playing at such events. My mother milked about a dozen cows and sold the milk and cream for extra dollars. It took perseverance, tenacity, hard work, and bravery to survive the Great Depression and their living conditions at that time.

When the Second World War broke out in 1939, living became even more challenging as there was rationing of all types of goods. Gasoline, sugar, butter, to name a few, were only obtained with coupons. The Government issued coupons, allotting each person or family a rationed amount of items that could be bought. Everyone was treated equally; gasoline coupons were issued to all Canadians, even if you didn't own a vehicle. Our family did not have a car and were able to trade their gas coupons for either sugar or butter coupons. We made our own butter on the farm, so mostly the gas and butter coupons were bartered for sugar and some other rationed items. Growing up, observing how my parents bravely lived through these difficult times rubbed off on me and my brothers, we all were entrepreneurs—knowing that if you were brave enough then you could survive and even make progress by welcoming each new day with enthusiasm and living each day with a positive attitude and never giving up.

School, for me, was great. I loved to learn and wanted to be the best in class, in all my grades. From Grade 1 until I left Sandy Lake, I was never lower that third. I was very competitive and strived for first in class. Second was okay, but being third—I was disappointed. I competed against two others who were a lot smarter than I; as a result, I worked harder so that I would be in the top three in each particular grade.

We played hockey in winter on an open air rink located next to our school, and, many times during recess or at lunch time, the boys would go and clear the snow off the ice so we could practice skating and played hockey at night. In the summer, we played baseball. My brothers and I were involved in drama in town, plays were put on either at school or at the churches in town, and we were quite active, especially in Ukrainian dancing. I know that my childhood was wonderful, but going out into the world and becoming an adult changes everything.

On July 7, 1999, I was leaving for Edmonton on a business trip. As I was getting ready to leave at 5:00 a.m., I noticed some blood in the toilet after my morning bowel movement. I didn't have any pain and dismissed it as nothing serious. On the trip, I had to use the toilet again in Red Deer and blood was again noticeable. All throughout the day, while making my sales calls, I had to use the toilet several times and each time there was blood. That evening, when I checked into my hotel, I took off my necktie, hung up my clothes, and sat on the toilet. This time, as I got up, I fell to the floor; I had passed out from the loss of blood. This occurred at about 5:00 p.m.; I was unconscious for about two hours. I eventually regained consciousness and dragged myself to the bed. I called my wife in Calgary and she told me to go to a hospital. I was reluctant and wanted to wait until next morning, and planned to drive back to Calgary and see my own doctor. My wife insisted that I go to a hospital. I took a taxi from my hotel to the University Hospital at about eight that evening. The emergency unit quickly started to investigate my problems and I was admitted and tests started. By morning I was stabilized and it was determined that I had a tumour in my intestines and surgery was slated for 10:00 a.m. They removed a two-and-a-half-pound malignant growth from the junction of my large and small intestines. They removed all the cancerous tissue near where the growth had been and I was then cancer free.

After a week in the hospital, I was sent home to Calgary in a wheelchair. During my time at the University Hospital, I was well taken care of. My luck was with me; we had lived in Edmonton from 1988 to 1993, so I had made some good friends. I was also lucky that the chief of staff at this hospital was the surgeon who headed up my surgical procedure to remove the cancerous tumour. Also, the head of nursing was a person who we had made friends with at the church that we attended when we were living in Edmonton prior to all this. Imagine the excellent attention I received from the nursing staff when the chief of staff of surgery and the head of nursing visited me on a daily basis. My friend the nurses' boss brought me a newspaper every morning. Plus, others from the church that we attended, some family members who resided in Edmonton, came to visit. I had plenty of visitors, but one thing I distinctly remember was a presence that was with me during the entire stay at the hospital. Even when there was no one else in the room with me, I felt that there was someone standing near me. I believe that it was God sending an angel to stand over me and to protect me. Perhaps it was my father, who had passed away some 40 years earlier. I don't know who or what it was, but I felt peaceful, brave, and strong. I knew that I would recover fully from this cancer journey. The pain from the surgery was there, but the pain-killing drugs and my belief in a full recovery made it all bearable. God gives us strength and the ability to be brave enough to overcome all adversity. Never give up.

Ignite your desire to become what you must be; live in a place of love and not fear.

No matter how young or old we are, or what your challenges are, live fearlessly by doing something positive for others and it will benefit us greatly.

- » Be brave, even when things are difficult.
- » Believe that you can succeed.
- » Know that if you begin, then you can win.
- » Do what scares you most.
- » Have the courage to live.
- » God sends people to help us overcome.
- » The biggest room in the world is room for improvement.
- » Believe in yourself.
- » Always be a friend.
- » Decide to feel good today, everyday.

YOU CAN'T WIN, IF YOU DON'T BEGIN

"DARE TO BE"
BY STEPHEN MARABOLI:

When a new day begins, dare to smile gratefully.

When there is darkness, dare to be the first to share a light.

When something seems difficult, dare to do it anyway.

When life seems to beat you down, dare to fight back.

When there seems to be no hope, dare to find some.

When you are feeling tired, dare to keep going.

When times are tough, dare to be tougher.

When love hurts you, dare to love again.

When someone is hurting, dare to help them heal.

When another is lost, dare to help them find the way.

When a friend falls, dare to be the first to extend a hand.

When you cross paths with another, dare to make them smile.

When you feel great, dare to help someone also feel great.

When the day has ended, dare to feel as if you've done your best.

Dare to be the best you can—but at all times, DARE TO BE.

Chapter 2
BECOME SOMEONE BUT BE YOURSELF

Moral virtues come from habit . . .
The habits we form from childhood make
no small difference, but rather make all the difference.   —Aristotle

You cannot make yourself feel something you do not want to feel,
but you can make yourself do the right thing in spite of your feelings.
                                        —Pearl S. Buck

Perseverance is another name for success.

A thankful person can find contentment anywhere.

Leisure activities help individuals to achieve balance,
relieve stress and foster a sense of well-being   —Jackie Webber

In all the trials that we experience, we do not realize how our character is developed, how our personalities are formed, what we become as result of the good times and the difficult events that we experience.

Being brave and taking a chance will always move us forward. Working hard at my schoolwork paid off. I was able to do my homework at the same time as other subjects were taught. For example, if I had Math homework, I would do it in the History class, and if History homework was assigned, I would do in Geography. As a result, I had very little homework to do at home in the evenings. This made me somewhat special with a few of the teachers. Starting in about Grade 4 or 5, I was doing well in school. One particular teacher treated me special. She was very encouraging, and many years later she told me that she tried not to have any favourites, but I was her "Teacher's Pet." Knowing that I was well liked made me feel like I was someone.

After leaving school, I had several jobs in and around home. My first job was for a local garage in town, cutting the ends out of old hot water tanks and welding them together creating culverts for the roads in the municipality. I lasted about three weeks, as I didn't get proper training and the bright light from the Arc Welder burned the retina of my eyes and I was confined to a dark room with severe pain and limited eyesight for almost a month. Next job was for a farmer quite a distance from our home. He was fairly large farmer and also raised show horses. I worked for a full summer and came home with some cash and also a team of matching show horses for my dad and the money went to my mom.

In that first winter after leaving school, I worked for a local contractor, on the ice gang, cutting ice on the lake into large blocks, loading them into Canadian National Railway cars and then going to various division points in Manitoba and Saskatchewan to unload all that ice into ice houses. This ice was used in passenger rail cars for drinking water. Here, too, I was treated well by the boss, and I got along well with the others in the work crew. I did everything that was expected of me and a little bit more. This showed that even though I was a teenager, I was able to keep up with the big guys and was treated as someone special.

In the numerous jobs that I have had, it seems that there was always someone there for me, a MENTOR. In each company, one person came to ensure that I had someone to help me develop good habits and to learn about the work and how to always do it to the best of my ability. I was taught that if you have a job to do, DO IT WELL.

In all the experiences of growing up and starting to work, some of the best lessons I learned were at home on the farm. In the 1930s and 1940s, almost all the work on the farms was done with horsepower, real horses, very few machines were available. Everybody pitched in and we all learned that each had chores to do and to help out whenever and wherever there was work to be done. My parents didn't force us to work, but it was just a given that each had to pull their weight, with no complaining, whining, or excuses.

We were taught to be ourselves, not to be aloof or think that were above anyone. It was instilled in us to "Be Yourself." I recall being told that, "You are special; there is no one else in the world like you," especially by my grandma who lived with us in the same yard. Grandma was one of the smartest people I know; she could only speak Ukrainian, but she told us that we were the smartest, best behaved, and best looking boys. And, as a result, we tried to live up this high standard she had set for us. How could we disappoint her, and I think that is why we didn't do anything to make her see us in a poor light.

The easiest way to feel good about oneself is to BE YOURSELF, this way a person doesn't appear as a phony. So the best advice we got from our parents and grandparents was to be yourself and be someone. Also, unless you have a good memory, it is best not to tell lies. Take responsibility for the consequences of your actions.

On November 20, 1947, when I was in Grade 7 at Sandy Lake School, my favourite teacher, Tillie Karliski, wrote this in my Autograph book:

Dear Tommy,
Life is like a mirror,
Reflecting what you do,
And if you face it smiling,
It smiles right back at you.

Sincerely,
Tillie Karliski

She was my most favourite teacher, and I have stayed in touch with her over the years.

Her words and the way she encouraged her students had a profound and positive impact on my life.

There were others who were my mentors: Bill Brokke at Rogers Fruit Company, Bill Tyson at Sunkist, Bill Tamagi at Bridge Brand, and Frank Gatto at V. G. Services.

How many people can you recall in your lifetime who helped you when you needed it?

Who was there encouraging you, advising and teaching you? Who set great examples for you to copy and follow? I am certain that everyone of us has had those wonderful individuals who moulded us into the successes we are today.

Have you helped anyone to be better, shared your knowledge and experience with them? There are a few in my life. Mark Tompkins at Sunkist moved up through the company and tells me that because of the teaching and helping that I gave to him enabled him to get become National Sales Manager. He went from a boy from Creston, B.C., to that position with a world-renowned organization. Rene Drouin in Montreal went from Merchandiser to District Manager of Canada's bilingual office. There are others who have gone on to bigger and better careers, owing to the encouragement and support that we can give. Recently, Shawna Taylor, an accountant working diligently at her craft, started volunteering, taking on a responsible position on a board and now wants to volunteer on additional boards, helping others.

Be a mentor to someone. We all know individuals who are our favourites. Help them by first becoming their friend and then encourage them to be a SOMEONE in their life.

HERE ARE THE PEOPLE IN MY LIFE WHO MOTIVATED AND INSPIRED ME:

Mary Shindruk, Mother
Bill Shindruk, Father
Sophia Shindruk, Grandmother
Bob Shindruk, Brother
Lloyd Shindruk, Brother
Sonja (Hullick) Shindruk, Wife
Kay Hullick, Mother-in-law
Bill Hullick, Father-in-Law
Tillie Karliski, Teacher
Bill Brokke, Boss
Bill Tyson, Boss
Rick Shindruk, Son
Randal Shindruk, Son
Tracy Katherine Mary Shindruk, Daughter
Pat Ochitwa, Friend
Junaid Malik,: Friend
Mona Cooley, Friend
Joyce Frandle, Friend
Shawna Taylor, Friend
Helen Cowie, Friend
Frank Gatto, Friend
Ed Demchuk, Friend
Dan Holinda - Friend

These people, and quite a few more, too many to mention, have had a profound effect on me throughout my life. The hundreds of people who I met over the last 84 years have made a profound difference in my life, some very positive, some less, and some more, and a few that made me make decisions not to be like them. Many made me feel like SOMEONE.

HOW CAN YOU HELP SOMEONE BECOME A SOMEONE?

- » There is only one of you and you are special.
- » There is no one else who looks like you—you are unique.
- » You cannot be like someone else.
- » Make others feel special.
- » Help someone to be better.
- » Be a MENTOR.
- » Bring out the best in others.
- » Share your talents and knowledge.
- » Each person has an incredible story to tell.

CHOOSE A JOB YOU LOVE AND YOU WILL NEVER HAVE TO WORK A DAY IN YOUR LIFE —CONFUCIUS

TOM SHINDRUK

Chapter 3
LEARN ALL YOU CAN

Man's mind stretched to a new idea never
goes back to its original dimensions.   *—Oliver Wendell Holmes Sr.*

Work joyfully and peacefully, knowing that right thoughts
and right efforts will inevitably bring about right results.

—James Allen

Mistakes are merely steps up the ladder.   —Paul J. Meyer

I was always curious about everything—I wanted to know as much as possible—and thereby I perhaps have this desire to read books. My work in the citrus industry gave me an opportunity to learn about farming in California, to know about the various varieties and characteristics of the different citrus fruits, their diseases and nutritive values. I wanted to learn all about marketing and merchandizing, and, as a result, I got to not only be somewhat of an expert in the citrus world, but also to travel all over Canada and the United States. The 18 years in the citrus business were the best years of my life: I was young, married to a wonderful woman, had great children, and was proud to work hard to take care of my family. My work world started in the 1950s, and my careers took me to various places, with transfers and being in my own business.

Here are the jobs titles I have had and the companies I have worked for over the years:

1950	Welder, summer job at Tony Kellers Garage
1951	Farm Hand, summer job for Taras Kristolovich
1952	Ice Gang Labourer, winter job for Pete Hnatiuk
1953	Sheet Metal Worker, Selkirk Metal Products, Winnipeg
1953	Warehouse, Truck Driver, and Sales, Rogers Fruit Company, Winnipeg
1957	Merchandiser, Supervisor, Trainer, District Manager, Sunkist Growers, Winnipeg, Toronto, Cleveland, and Calgary
1975	Owner/Manager, Alexandra Hotel, Drumheller
1980	Realtor, Lyall Real Estate, Calgary
1982	Sales Manager, Pak-Wel Produce, Vauxhall
1984	Vice President Sales and Marketing, V. G. Services Ltd., Vauxhall
1986	Sales Manager, Bridge Brand Food Services, Calgary
1988	Sales Manager, Mustang Food Brokerage, Edmonton
1993	Realtor, Sutton Real Estate, Calgary
1995	Vice-President Marketing, V. G. Services Ltd, Calgary
2000	President and Owner, Trason Marketing, Calgary
2004	Vice-President Workplace Health & Safety, Alberta Food Processors Association

2008	Classroom Trainer, Fleet Safety International (FSI), Calgary
2008	Facilitator—Be a Great Dad Program, Families Matter, Calgary
2016	Sales Representative, i-Group of Companies
2017	Sales Agent, Liquidity Services
2017	Max & Property Services - Agent
2019	eLearning Max - Sales Representative
2020	Counter Intelligence Services - Agent

Presently, I am working part time at both FSI and Families Matter, and, of course, I am volunteering.

Volunteering is also something that I have been doing for a very long time, since beating cancer three times. I have been involved with the Canadian Cancer Society as a volunteer and lately as a Board Member—learning about the numerous types of cancer, prevention, and treatments; speaking for about 10 years to whomever would listen to me; and serving on various committees, such as, Agriculture and Food Council, Oakfield Park Villas Condominium Association, Sabrina Way Condo Association, Calgary Academy of Chefs, Canadian Blood Services, and Developmental Disabilities Resource Foundation and their Centre.

Each time I volunteered, I learned more about these wonderful organizations that do so much for others. Helping people as much as you can and not expecting anything in return is the best feeling in the world. By this I mean doing for others and learning about running boards, governance, about parliamentary procedures, about doing good for others, and making a difference in the world, because, when we help others, we are making a difference in THEIR world. Do something nice for someone and try not to get caught.

Today, at his stage of my life, at the age of 84, I am still active in the work world, doing classroom training at Fleet Safety International, mostly in the Oil and Gas Industry. My other job is with Families Matter, where I am a facilitator, doing the Be a Great Dad program, helping fathers to be better dads, husbands, and men. These two jobs are the best I have ever had, and it takes a lot of reading, researching on the Internet, listening to others, and learning all that I can to be good at the work that I so love to do.

How do I know how to do all of this? By learning all I can about the subjects that I teach.

In the volunteer world, I am Chairman of the Board at DDRC, Board Member at the Canadian Cancer Society, Member of the Advisory Council at Canadian Blood Services, Lifetime Member of the Calgary Academy of Chefs, Past Chairman of the Value Chain Action Committee at Agriculture, and Food Council, Member of AGFC for seven years,

I am the Past President of the Oakfield Park Villas Condominium Association, and currently Board Member of Sabrina Way Condo Association. My advice? Keep learning all the time.

How do I find time to work two jobs and volunteer with all these organizations and still have time for myself and for my wife and family? I don't know how it works, but it seems that the more time I give to others, the more time I seem to have for myself as well.

In 2004, the Canadian Cancer Society presented the "Certificate of Appreciation" award to me. In 2006, I received the "Distinguished Service" award. In 2010, the CCS gave me the "Distinguished Community Engagement" award, and, in 2013, I was again honoured by getting the "National Impact Award of Courage."

The Canadian Cancer Society nominated me for the "QUEEN ELIZABETH DIAMOND JUBILEE" award in 2013.

In 2017, the Canadian Cancer Society nominated me for the "ORDER OF CANADA," and Families Matter nominated me for the "TOP 70 OVER 70" award.

HOW DOES ONE GET THE KNOWLEDGE NEEDED FOR SUCCESS? HERE IS WHAT NEEDS TO BE DONE:

» Learn all you can—knowledge is power.
» Do all you can, as much as you can, for as many as you can.
» Do everything that is expected of you and just a little bit more.
» Help others and expect nothing in return.
» Be reliable, show up on time, and use everything that you have learned about the work you do.
» Be friendly and treat everyone with respect.
» Maintain a positive attitude.
» Learn to love your job; fake it until you make it.
» Smile and say Please and Thank You a lot.
» Listen more than talk.

TEN TIPS FOR TAKING
CONTROL OF YOUR TIME

1. List everything you need to do today, in order of priority.
2. Make time for important things, not just urgent ones.
3. Write your goals, then write the steps to your goals.
4. Set a starting time as well as a deadline for all projects.
5. Slice up big projects into bite-size pieces.
6. If you run out of steam on one project, switch to another.
7. Say no to new projects when you're already overloaded.
8. Trim low-payoff activities from your schedule.
9. For each paper that crosses your desk, act on it, file it, or toss it.
10. Use a Day-Timer system to manage your busy life.

Chapter 4
ALWAYS BUILD—
DON'T DESTROY

Always be kinder than necessary. —James M Barrie

He only profits from praise that values criticism. —Heinrich Heine

Whatever you are, be a good one. —Abraham Lincoln

I've never seen a monument erected to a pessimist. —Paul Harvey

In the early sixties, I was Merchandizing Supervisor in the citrus business and was a trainer in New York. When the company had hired at least eight new people, they would be brought to New York for two weeks of product knowledge and merchandising training. The Fruit Auction on Pier 52 afforded us the ability to show the new trainees the types of citrus that were grown. This was a great location to teach the new employees about the various characteristics and qualities of the oranges, lemons, and grapefruits from the different growing areas of California and Arizona. I was one of the trainers, and the gentleman who was the Eastern Division Manager was the most amazing man, teacher, mentor, and friend. He usually gave the final wrap-up after the new hires were put through the classroom work, did the early morning visits to observe the activities in the Auction, and also did the inspection of the citrus displayed on the floor for the buyers to look at before the bidding began. At one of these training session, his theme was "ALWAYS BUILD, DON'T DETROY," and that phrase has stuck with me for over 60 years. His message is that, as humans, we live with others on this planet and we should always build others. Pay someone a compliment at every opportunity. Praise someone at every chance we get. Make others feel important. Tell people how important they are to us. Tell those close to you, how much you love them; show your love, especially your family. Make others feel good about themselves. This is so easy to do. And when we build others, we build ourselves. Compliment others on their attire, their hair; everyone loves to hear praise. Tell someone how much you like their tie, sweater, shirt, suit, shoes (especially if they are clean and shiny)—anything that might make them feel good about themselves. And if they do something well, tell them how proud you are to work with such efficient people. Everyone loves PRAISE. Do it often and to as many as you can.

Here's what the Pope said recently:

> Stop being negative. "Needing to talk badly about others indicates low self-esteem. That means, 'I feel so low that instead of picking myself up I have to cut others down,'" the Pope said. "Letting go of negative things quickly is healthy."

If you hang around with negative people long enough, it's likely you'll become more negative yourself. Stay out of areas at work where all you encounter are gripe sessions. Find positive people to spend time with. Sometime in 2000, I met two people who changed my life: Junaid Malik and Mona Cooley. I met Junaid at a Toastmasters Convention. I was giving the Keynote Address at the wrap up of a full day of training.

Junaid was then working at the Canadian Cancer Society in charge of Fund Raising. Junaid approached me and asked for a copy of my speech. Because it was written on the back of an envelope and a few scraps of paper, I gave him the notes. Apparently, he was so impressed that he convinced me to join the Canadian Cancer Society as a volunteer, and we became lifelong friends. I also met Mona Cooley through Toastmasters, and she, Junaid, and I formed a Mentorship Group.

For many years, the three of us met quite often, shared our challenges and successes, bounced our problems off each other, and generally came up with solutions.

We inspired each other and we have continued to do so now for almost 15 years. Each of us believe that life should be wonderful, in spite of the daily challenges that we all face. We all differ in age: Junaid is about one-third my age, Mona is about one-half my age, and yet we all find that we all have knowledge, ideas, and solutions to almost anything that we have ever faced., We are constantly learning. Always striving to be better than we used to be.

Henry Ford said, "Anyone who stops learning is old, whether at twenty or eighty."

If you can, start a dialogue between your co-workers or your friends, where you share life's challenges, help each other to find solutions. I read a statement by an anonymous person: "The wise don't expect to find life worth living, they make it that way." And I firmly believe that we all have knowledge that should be shared.

TO BUILD OTHERS AND YOURSELF:

» Always build—don't destroy.

» Say nice things to all you meet.

» Do something for someone else and expect nothing in return.

» Be encouraging to those who are struggling.

» Maintain a POSITIVE ATTITUDE at all times.

» Smile, even if you don't feel like it.

» Look and act like you are successful.

» You can't put a price on what you do for others.

BRING ME ALL YOUR FLOWERS NOW

I would rather have a single rose
from the garden of a friend,
than have the choicest flowers,
when my stay on earth must end.

I would rather have the kindest words
which may now be said to me
than flattered when my heart is still
and this life has ceased to be.

I would rather have a single smile
from friends I know are true
than tears shed 'round my casket.
when this world I bid adieu.

Bring me all your flowers,
whether pink, or white, or red,
I'd rather have one blossom now—
THAN A TRUCKLOAD WHEN I'M DEAD!

Chapter 5
DO WHAT YOU FEAR MOST

Whatever your hand finds to do,
do it with all your might. —Ecclesiastes 9;10 NIV

Find a purpose in life so big it will challenge
every capacity to be at your best. —David O. McKay

Enthusiasm and persistence can make an average person superior;
indifference and lethargy can make a superior person average.
—William A. Ward

Keep trying. It's only from the valley that the mountain seems high.

To be a real champion, you must believe you are the best.
If you're not, pretend you are. —Muhammad Ali

FEAR—False Evidence Appears Real.

Fear is sometimes not real. How many times have we worried about what might happen and how we would handle it if it did. I know, years ago, I would stay up all night, couldn't fall asleep, and would worry about what might happen. Then, in the morning, after a sleepless night of tossing and turning, looking tired, you find out that NOTHING happened and all that stress was for nothing. In the many jobs that I have held, many were quite stressful, and then adding unwarranted worry created so much stress that sometimes I couldn't think straight. We make poor decisions many times when we are stressed out. It took me many years to give up worrying about stuff that had not happened. My journey with cancer four times was painful, mostly because of surgery, chemo, and radiation. I was able to compose myself and maintained a positive attitude. I just knew that I would survive, that I would beat cancer. Since 1999, when I was stricken with cancer and had major surgery to remove a two-and-a-half-pound tumour from the junction of my large and small intestines, I told everyone that I was going to be fine. During the second bout, in 2001, when the prostate cancer was detected and hormonal treatment was applied, I also felt that this was just a minor inconvenience and I planned to get rid of the cancer and get on with life. In 2004, when the prostate cancer returned and the decision was made to take 38 radiation treatments, I, too, just knew that I would overcome it and live. All the treatments to get the cancer killed is very hard on the physical body. Think how much could also happen to someone when they don't believe in their physicians and (or) the treatments. In many ways, I believe that cancer was a Blessing for me. Because of my journey with cancer, I was able to do so many things in my life that I probably would not have even attempted, if I had not had the big "C." I never gave up. In 2017 the doctors found a growth on my right kidney and at first it was thought to be cancer however it has been determined that it is a benign tumour and so we are in a watch and wait mode checking it every six months.

Constantly being fearful and worried can compromise the immune system, and that just allows the diseases to attack the organs in our bodies. Mentally, one must strongly work at being positive about what life gives us. We will not get through life without stress. At some time during our days here on earth, we will experience personal problems, sicknesses, and challenges that will test our ability to deal with them in a calm and wise way. Worrying does not help. For many years, I was a worrier; I told everyone that my mother was a worrier, and I was one, too. I really had to work at changing the way I looked at life and then handle it in a way that was not stressing me out. It can be done. Having a spouse that loves and supports you also can be a great healing. Believe in the medical systems, the medicines and treatments, and, more importantly, have faith in God. It works best for me and can work for you, too. Never give up.

Use the power of your mind. In November and December of 2004, while I was being treated for prostate cancer, I was given 38 radiation treatments. The procedure is not painful: the nurses strap you down on a (cold) table and you must lie completely still. The procedure takes about 20 minutes, to get you ready, undressed, positioned, and strapped down. The actual radiation only lasts about three minutes. Then the sound of the radiation machine starts. I pictured the cancer cells in my body like soap bubbles, and as the machine whirred, the bubbles kept bursting. This went on for 37 treatment times, and on the last day of my radiation treatments, the 38th, there were no more bubbles. The cancer was gone, and, to date, has not returned. Recent PSA tests were at .03, which indicates no cancer. The power of the mind is amazing: use it, visualize, and you will see what happens before it happens.

The support of your spouse, family, and friends is also so comforting and important. The number of people who have prayed and (or) are praying for me is hard to count, but they are many. Not only did my wife believe that I would be cured of cancer, she also didn't say or do anything that might discourage me. Confirming that we can get through the everyday challenges with help from your spouse and children gives one HOPE in living through these challenging and scary events. But remember, NEVER GIVE UP.

HOW TO RESIST FEAR:

- » Stop worrying—it does not help.
- » Resist all negative thoughts and feelings.
- » Surround yourself with positive people.
- » Stay healthy; even when you're sick, do all you can to eat HEALTHILY.
- » Exercise on a regular basis, at least 5 times per week, and consume only foods that will enhance your health.
- » Don't worry about things that have not happened.
- » Be good to yourself and to all you meet.

A SPECIAL LOVE LETTER

You say you love me, but sometimes you don't show it. In the beginning, you could not do enough for me. Now you seem to take me for granted. Some days I wonder if I mean anything to you at all.

Maybe when I'm gone you'll appreciate me and all the things I do for you. I'm responsible for the food on your table, for the clothes that you wear, for the welfare of your home, for the thousand and one things that you want and need. Why, if it wasn't for me, you wouldn't have the car that you drive.

I've kept quiet and waited to see how long it would take for you to realize how much you really need me.

Cherish me . . . take good care of me . . . and I'll take good care of you.

Who am I?

I'm your job.

Chapter 6
NEVER GIVE UP: ALL THINGS ARE POSSIBLE

*It takes just as much faith to believe you are going
to fail as it takes to believe you are going to succeed.*　　—unknown

*We make a living by what we get,
but we make a life by what we give.*　　—Winston Churchill

*Our thanksgiving today should include
those things which we take for granted.*　　—Betty Fuhrman

Too many individuals don't have staying power. They give up too soon. Success comes to people who hang in and don't give up. How many of us wish for something and then fail to start. Not getting started is the big problem, saying that someday I will get to it, someday I will do this or that, but it never happens. Someday I will take a vacation to some exotic location, but, not saving for it, it doesn't happen. How many individuals want to start their own business but keep wishing and get old and never make their dreams come true. Starting something is something half done.

If we fear doing something, but we should just do it. My fear of public speaking was so bad that my mouth would get dry, I felt sweaty, and my knees went weak. I was called on to make presentations in most of my work, especially in my early days in the citrus business.

I took a Public Speaking course in the first year that I was employed by Sunkist. This helped me overcome some of my fears, but I still didn't have the confidence that I felt I needed to be good at speaking. I would accept any opportunity to act as an MC, and people told me that I was quite good at it; however, I still felt I was not that good at it. I joined TOASTMASTERS and that increased my confidence and speaking ability. Today, I am a Motivational Speaker, Facilitator, and I can speak with confidence at any event and on any subject. I was terrified to speak without notes. Today, I prefer to speak without notes, and it works well. Believe in yourself, but, more importantly, persevere; keep on doing what you fear the most and you will overcome your fear. Also, be grateful for all opportunities. Most challenges and problems are just opportunities in disguise.

During the 1960s, while we were living in Toronto, I was with Sunkist and was appointed Supervisor of the Merchandizing Division and was the trainer. This called on me to travel all over Canada and the United States. This was a great learning experience for me, working with people of all ages; some of the managers in the offices in North America were more than twice my age. The newly hired employees were about my age or a bit younger, and the staff in the 55 offices in North America varied in age. I had to adjust my thoughts and technique in my dealing with the staff in each office. Attitude played a big role in my dealings with all of these various people; their character and personalities were all different. Not only did I have to act mature, polished, and knowledgeable, I had to look it. Sunkist had strict rules in their dress code. Suits, white shirts, and ties. Shoes had to be shiny, clothes clean. I recall going to Washington, D.C., to train a brand new employee. He was to meet me at the airport, but I didn't know what he looked like and he didn't know me. He asked the District Manager of the local office how would he recognize me and was told to look for the guy with the shiniest shoes departing the plane, that will be Tom. Dress for success—look like you are successful. Appearance is vital, especially in business, but it is also important in our personal life. Remember, "We rarely get a second chance to make a first good impression."

Beating cancer is all about never giving up. In 2011, owing to some of the procedures that the doctors used to remove the tumour from my stomach in 1999, I started to bleed internally and was losing blood through the bowel. I was rushed to the hospital and spent a week there before the problems was corrected. Immediately, the doctors knew that my situation was dire. I was losing blood so fast that my body was not able to replace it. I collapsed in the emergency room and the staff jumped into action. I was the centre of the urgency to save my life. In the first three days of my stay at the hospital, I was given nine units of blood and they did not determine what the problems was, where was I bleeding from, and what they needed to do to correct the bleeding. That was not ever determined. During my stay that week, and especially on the second day. After about the seventh unit of blood, I was in a room with three other patients, two men and a woman. As I lay there that night, with the room in almost total darkness, I was awake and started to feel sorry for myself. As I silently cried, listening to the laboured breathing of the sick people in that room, I started to pray, and I asked God to heal me and to give me a sign of some kind, any kind that I would be okay or that He would give some kind of message of what I had to do. I scanned the ceiling tiles in that darkened room waiting for a message, but none came. I must have fallen asleep, because when I awoke, it came to me that I had to do something to ensure that others would live just as I was given another chance with the blood that was administered to keep me alive. Then my mind started working: how can

I do this? I prayed for guidance and the ideas started flowing. I thought that if I required nine units to save my life, how many others at this time in this same hospital needed blood to stay alive. I asked to speak with the nurse in charge of the unit that I was in. I spoke with her about my plan, and she suggested that she would set up a meeting with the hospital administrator. My plan was to help by volunteering with Canadian Blood Services (CBS) and get as many organizations and people that I knew to donate blood on a regular basis. When my wife came to visit me, I got her to start calling a few of our friends and ask them to come to the hospital for a meeting with me. I also asked the hospital to set up a command centre for me where I would have access to a phone and computer. By the end of that day, I was moved to a private room with everything that I had requested. Then the managers, owners, and key people in my group of friends and others who would have influence were summoned to my hospital room and the plan was formed to get the word out that everyone should give blood and save a life. It is amazing how quickly things can happen if you ASK and just start doing things. As a result of this episode with the urgent need for blood I was able to start a movement that added to what the CBS are already doing. I am now on the Advisory Council for Alberta and Northwest Territories at CBS. and attend meetings to review the strategies and assist where needed to ensure that there is an adequate supply of blood for people that need it. This event where I almost died has changed my life, by doing something for others. Do everything that needs to be done and then just do a little bit more and your life will be extraordinary.

I love what Ron Southern, Chairman of Atco, wrote, and it is posted at most Atco Companies on their bulletin boards:

"EXCELLENCE—Going far beyond the call
of duty. Doing more than others expect. This is

what excellence is all about. It comes from striving, maintaining the highest standards, looking for the smallest details and going that extra mile. Excellence means caring. It means making a special effort to do more."

IF YOU WANT SUCCESS IN YOUR LIFE, THEN DO THE FOLLOWING:

» Dress for success
» Strive for excellence
» Volunteer—do something for someone else and ask for nothing in return.
» Love everyone.
» Make your WISH come true, by wishing for it, wanting it, and working at it.
» Start something—don't procrastinate.
» Do everything that is required of you and just a little bit more.
» NEVER GIVE UP.

CHILDREN LEARN WHAT THEY LIVE

If a child lives with criticism.
    he learns to condemn.

If a child lives with hostility,
    he learns to fight.

If a child lives with ridicule,
    he learns to be shy.

If a child lives with shame,
    he learns to feel guilty.

If a child lives with tolerance,
    he learns to be patient.

If a child lives with encouragement,
    he learns confidence.

If a child lives with praise,
    he learns to appreciate.

If a child lives with security,
    he learns to have faith.

If a child lives with approval,
    he learns to like himself.

If a child lives with acceptance and friendship,
    he learns to find love in the world.

TOM SHINDRUK

Chapter 7
BE HAPPY AND STAY POSITIVE

Do not let the sun go down
while you are still angry. —Ephesians 4;26 NIV

Teach me, Father, to value each day,
to live, to love, to laugh, to play. —Kathi Mills

Beauty will mould each thought that lives
within me— I shall remember only lovely things. —Willa Hoey

You can't give away kindness. It always comes back.

Every little blessing is far too precious
to ever forget to say "THANK YOU."

How can we have a wonderful and happy life? How can we love what we do to make a living? There have been many books written on this, and like taking a course on Time Management, there is good advice, but then life interferes with our dreams and wishes.

So many people complain about their work, their job, their fellow workers, and the weather.

Oh, yes, the list goes on, and how much good does it do to complain? Then how many individuals who we know are never satisfied, and say negative things, such as, "It's too cold today," or "It's too hot," or "Too windy," "There is not even a breeze today." Yes, we all know someone whot is never happy with anything, or says things, such as , "I hate this," or "I hate her or him." These are words that express negativity. Would it not be better to perhaps use different language? Would substituting the word "HATE" with a better designation for how we feel by substituting it with words, for example, "I'm just not pleased with this cold snap, but this will not last and eventually it will warm up."

Or we could also say this, "I am not too fond of so and so" instead of "I hate him."

There is always a better choice of words that we can use to create a better feeling around us, to create a much more positive atmosphere when we communicate with others. And it doesn't matter if it's family, fellow workers, friends or anyone we meet. Start using words that indicate a positive climate. In everything we do, we have a choice in how we do things, how we react to what is happening to us or to others.

In our complex where we now live, we have 54 condo units, and most of the homeowners plant flowers in their front yards. This year, one of our neighbours came and helped herself to a handful of very aromatic smelling sweet peas from our front yard without asking permission. Instead, she came to our door with a handful of sweet peas and simply said that I hope you don't mind that I helped myself to your sweet peas. How did we react? We said, "Oh, it's okay."

What we really wanted to say was, "No, it is not okay. Why don't you plant your own flowers so you don't have to take from our garden," but we didn't say that. Probably, what would be the best thing to do would be, next spring, buy a packet of sweet peas seeds and give it to our neighbour and tell her that because she loved our sweet peas so much last year we want her to have her own to enjoy in her own flower garden this coming summer.

Every time we say something when we are angry or upset, we usually say something that we later regret or need to apologize for. The best that we can do is to not get upset or angry, and I know that is very difficult. Others do things and say things that could easily make us angry. Well, the best thing you can do is don't take it personally. Also, if someone makes you angry, forgive him or her immediately. If we let things that someone said or did fester and we keep telling others what was said about you, or done to you, we are just keeping the event alive. Let it die, by forgetting it and forgiving the perpetrator. Let go and let God.

Be happy, be grateful, and be thankful at all times and about everything in your life. Certainly, there will be times when you are not pleased or satisfied with how your life is going. Then start to think about all the good stuff that you have. In fact, it is a good idea to make a list of your blessings. Do you have a job? Do you have place to live? Do you have food? Do you have clothes? Do you have someone who loves you?

I read somewhere that if you have some loose change in your pocket, you're luckier that several billion people on the earth. Almost all of us living here in Canada have opportunities to get whatever we want, to go anywhere we want, and do whatever we want.

This is a free country, rated as one of the best countries in the world to live. Our opportunities are unlimited here. We can change jobs if we don't like where we are. If we don't like our boss or the salary we are paid, we can look for something better. Some of the jobs I had were great; however, some were not good. In most cases, when I was not happy with the place I was working, I acted like I was happy and at the same time I was looking for another position. In other words, Fake It. No one knew that I was so unhappy, and they didn't suspect that I was looking for another job. The same is true regarding people with whom we are not impressed; the best thing to do is act like you think they are okay. We cannot be close friends with everyone we meet, so, as a result, only cultivate friendships with the ones we like. Eventually, the ones we don't want to be our friends will get the message.

Act like you are happy all the time and you will cultivate and develop a happy attitude. Your life will take on an aura that others will wish they could have. Have good manners and dress like you are successful.

WHAT CAN WE DO TO BE HAPPY?

» Be thankful for what we have.
» Shake off any and all feelings of anger.
» Look toward to the future with optimism.
» Know that you are special; there is no one else in the world like you.
» Learn to like yourself; how can we expect others to like us if we don't like us.
» Do something for others—volunteer.
» Keep yourself healthy—exercise and eat nutritious foods.
» Pay someone a compliment—make someone feel good.

YOU ARE BLESSED

» If you own just one Bible… You are abundantly blessed. One-third of the world does not have access to one.
» If you woke up this morning with more health than illness… You are more blessed than the millions who will not survive this week.
» If you have never experiences the danger of battle, the loneliness of imprisonment, the agony of torture, or the pangs of starvation… You are ahead of 500 million people in the world.

TOM SHINDRUK

» If you can attend a church meeting without fear of harassment, arrest, torture, or death... You are more blessed than three billion people in the world.

» If you have food in the refrigerator, clothes on your back, a roof over your head, and a place to sleep... You are richer than 75% of the world.

» If you have money in the bank, in your wallet, and some spare change in a dish someplace... You are among the top eighth of the world's wealthy.

» If your parents are still alive and still married... You are very rare.

» If you hold up your head with a smile on your face and are truly thankful... You are blessed because the majority can, but do not.

» If you can hold someone's hand, hug them, or even touch them on the shoulder... You are blessed because you can offer God's healing touch.

» If you prayed yesterday and today... You are in the minority because you believe God hears and answers prayers.

» If you believe in Jesus as the son of God... You are part of a small minority in the world.

» If you can read this message... You are more blessed than over two billion people in the world who cannot read at all.

THE MAGIC BANK ACCOUNT

Imagine that you have won the following *PRIZE* in a contest: Each morning, your bank would deposit $86,400 in your private account for your use. However, this prize has rules: The set of rules:

1. Everything that you didn't spend during each day would be taken away from you.
2. You may not simply transfer money into some other account.
3. You may only spend it.
4. Each morning, upon awakening, the bank opens your account with another $86,400 for that day.
5. The bank can end the game without warning; at any time it can say, "Game Over!" It can close the account and you will not receive a new one. What would you personally do? You would buy anything and everything you wanted, right? And you would buy not only for yourself but also for all the people you love and care for. You would even buy for people you don't know, because you couldn't possibly spend it all on yourself, right? You would try to spend every penny, and use it all, because you knew it would be replenished in the morning, right? ACTUALLY, this GAME is REAL ... Shocked??? YES! Each of us is already a winner of this *PRIZE*. We just can't seem to see it. The PRIZE is *TIME*.

1. Each morning, we awaken to receive 86,400 seconds, as a gift of life.
2. And when we go to sleep at night, any remaining time is Not credited to us.
3. What we haven't used up that day is forever lost.
4. Yesterday is forever gone.

5. Each morning the account is refilled, but the bank can dissolve your account at any time WITHOUT WARNING ... SO, what will YOU do with your 86,400 seconds? Those seconds are worth so much more than the same amount in dollars. Think about it and remember to enjoy every second of your life, because time races by so much quicker than you think. So take care of yourself, be happy, love deeply, and enjoy life! Here's wishing you a wonderful and beautiful day. Start "spending" ... "DON'T COMPLAIN ABOUT GROWING OLD ...! SOME PEOPLE DON'T GET THE PRIVILEGE!"

The author is not known. It was found in the billfold of coach Paul Bear Bryant, Alabama, after he died in 1982.

Chapter 8
LEAVE A LEGACY

What can I give Him, poor as I am?
If I were a shepherd, I would bring a lamb;
If I were a Wise Man, I would do my part;
Yet what can I give Him: give my heart. —Christina Rosetti

The love we give away is the only love we keep. —Elbert Hubbard

The greatest of all mistakes is to do nothing
because you can do very little. Do what you can. —Sydney Smith

IF EVERYBODY WAS SATISFIED WITH
HIMSELF THERE WOULD BE NO HEROES. —Mark Twain

What are you doing here with your life that will make you and others happy? How do others view us? Will your family be proud of who you are and what you do? Everyone of us has parents, grandparents, siblings, and other extended family members and friends in our lives who leave an impression on us, either good or bad. These impressions start from a very young age. How was your life as a child? Did your parents stay married or were you brought up in a broken home. All of us are a reflection of what happened when we were very young. If the father was gentle and loving, then you as a son will in almost all cases be that way, too. However, if you lived with violence in the home, then you will probably also be a violent or angry person. This also applies to both genders: girls will usually become like their mothers and boys will usually turn out like their fathers.

Statistics tell us that children who have single parents could have major issues in growing up. Some will likely turn to drugs, crime, and have unwanted pregnancies. On the other hand, where there are two loving parents who live in harmony and show respect for each other, andhelp each other with household chores, they will set an example that their children will use later in their lives.

Reflecting back on our childhoods, do we remember how our parents conducted themselves in everyday living? How did your grandparents behave? Did they show love and respect for each other, for their families, and what type of people were their friends?

Who were friends with your family? Were they people with good morals?

Did they go to church? Did they treat others with kindness? If there was violence in the home, then there is a very high probability that this will carry on in the next generation.

What would we like our children to say to others about us as parents? How will they view us and what will they say about us at their weddings. Are we doing the right things and saying what would make our children proud of us? Will our children want to be like us?

What we do at home, at work, and at social functions, reflects our character and what we are all about. Leave a legacy of others respecting us and our children will want to be like us.

In the fall of 1988, I took on the position of manager of a food brokerage in Edmonton. I rented a small apartment as my family was still back in Calgary trying to sell our home. During this time, a friend suggested that I take a course called The Christopher Leadership Course. A friend was also one of the instructors, and it took 10 evenings to complete. The course covered a number of initiatives: Team Building, Networking, Spiritual, and the one that stands out the most for me was Change the World. When we were prompted to change the world, they mentioned Jonas Salk, who developed a vaccine for polio, Louis Pasteur, who developed the pasteurization process, Alexander Graham Bell, who invented the telephone, and Thomas Edison, who invented the lightbulb. I went home after that session and wracked my brain, but I didn't have a clue about what to do or what I could do the change the world. Certainly, I didn't have the intelligence or the ability to come up with anything even remotely close to those great men who were mentioned. I called my friend, the instructor, and explained my dilemma. He said, I know everybody has difficulty with this, and certainly most can't come up with some earth-shaking solution. He asked if there was some person who I could do something for that would change their world.

My mother lived in Manitoba and was battling bone cancer. She was in stage 4, which meant that she was not going to beat the disease. Mother was admitted to the Princess Elizabeth Hospital, and this is the hospice from which you are not coming home. She was very sick, couldn't carry on a long conversation, had problems writing, and mostly slept, owing to the strong pain killers that she was on. I had visited her a few weeks earlier, but the distance from Edmonton to Winnipeg meant that it could be months before I was able to see her again. Phone conversations were difficult for her, so I decided that I would write her a letter every week. I did this for over three months until she passed away. After her death, I went to Winnipeg for the funeral and visited the Princess Elizabeth Hospital. I bought the biggest box of chocolates that I could find and delivered it to the wing where my mother was taken care of. When I introduced myself, they told me that one letter had arrived just after she died. I was given that letter and was told that each letter that she received cheered her up and made a difference in her life. My weekly message from over a thousand miles away made a difference in my mother's world.

There are so many things that we can do to change the world for someone every day. Show your LOVE. A smile, a friendly gesture, a compliment—anything that will lift the spirits of others is not only a gift to them but also a gift to ourselves.

Dr. Wayne Dyer says, "There are three kinds of love":
1. Human Love—It changes and it varies.
2. Spiritual Love—It never changes but varies.
3. Divine Love—It never changes and never varies.

WHAT SHOULD WE DO TO LEAVE A LEGACY?

» Do what is right—forgive others and also forgive yourself.
» Don't be confrontational at home or anywhere else.
» Live a life by creating love and kindness.
» Treat others with respect.
» Show your LOVE for all, but especially to your spouse and children.
» Tell everyone how much they mean to you.
» Tell your spouse that you LOVE him or her all the time.
» Share the workload in the home.
» Do all you need to do and a little bit more.
» Be a great example of being a good provider for your family.
» Be a Hero to your family and others will see you as one.
» If you do more than you get paid for, you will eventually get paid more for than you do.

FRIENDSHIP ROAD

Friendship is a chain of gold,

Shaped in God's precious mould.

Each link is a smile, a laugh,

A tear, a grip of hand, a word of cheer.

As steadfast as the seasons roll.

Binding us closer, soul to soul.

No matter how far or heavy the load,

Sweet is the journey on friendship road.

Chapter 9
BE A POWER NETWORKER

We should not only use all the brains we have,
but all that we can borrow.

—Woodrow Wilson

Who is wise? He that learns from everyone.
Who is powerful? He that governs his passion.
Who is rich? He that is content.

—Benjamin Franklin

You learn something every day, if you pay attention. —Ray Lebrond

How many people do you know? Most of us have no idea how many individuals we have met in our lives, but more importantly, how many do we remember or remember us?

Early in my business life, when I was starting my career in the fresh produce industry, I was given some good advice from an old gentleman who was about to retire. He asked me if I wanted to be a success in the fresh fruit and vegetable business? I, of course, answered in the affirmative. Here is what I learned from this wise old man.

He explained that each of us meet new people every day, sometimes quite a few. At that time, I was a truck driver and delivered goods to grocery stores and restaurants in Winnipeg. It wasn't unusual for me to meet 15 to 20 new people every week. He told me to make one friend per week. He also explained that these friends do not necessarily have to visit you at your home or you at theirs, but you create a mutual admiration for each other, one that lasts for a long time. He instructed that I make one friend a week, and, in a year, I would have a minimum of 50 friends in the produce industry. He told me to do this for 10 years. If you have 500 friends in the business that you work in, you will not need any more friends and will be a success in that business. I never forgot that message and have lived my life of constantly meeting new people at every opportunity, and now I know people all over the world, with a huge following, not only in the food industry but also in all walks of life. I have saved every business card that I was ever given, and I have thousands still in boxes. During one of my recovery times, I went through them, and there were many people that I recalled who I had only met once; in fact, I recalled where and when and even some of the conversation. There were also some I worked with and couldn't recall what they looked like. Some of these networking contacts will impress us and some will not. Hang on to those that impress you and also those that are positive and add value to your life and to your work. When you know a great number of people, you have power. Make friends with everyone, no matter their station or position, because some of individuals in many companies will rise to more responsible positions and could become key managers. This means you have important people in places where major decisions are made, and remember, these are your friends. This makes life a lot easier, especially in business.

When I was transferred to Toronto in 1961, I met a young man, Roy Carson. He had immigrated from Ireland to Canada and was working as a produce clerk in a Dominion Store. I liked him immediately and he liked me. Within a short time, Roy was promoted to Produce Manager of that store. I built may displays in his store, which increased sales of oranges dramatically, so both he and I benefited from the promotional work that we did. Roy became Director of Purchasing for Dominion Stores in the head office in Toronto. I had a friend in a position where he had power in decision making and I had a product to sell. Did it help me as a salesperson to have someone that I respected and admired and call a friend? Of course it did. We all like to do business with people we like and trust.

If you want to become a Power Networker, read books about networking. In their book *Power Networking*, Donna Fisher and Sandy Vilas identified that there are "THREE P's of Networking." They are POWER, PEOPLE, and PROMOTION.

Anyone or everyone, regardless of age, educational degree, financial status, career path or geographic location, can do power networking. Realize that power networking is available to all, at least to anyone who is willing to consistently and extensively contribute to people through mutual sharing of knowledge and resources.

No matter what age, even at this time of my life at an advanced age, I still work every day to meet new people and to create a climate of mutual respect, where friendships are formed, and this helps to build business and realize numerous other benefits. However, be prepared to do something for the person in your network and get nothing in return. If we expect to get something back immediately, then this doesn't work. Don't worry if you give something, time or money or whatever; don't demand instant return. The benefits or return on the time or other investment will come back to us many times over.

Dr. Wayne Dyer says, "The people we meet in our lives, come to us for a reason, why? we don't know but eventually some of these individuals make a difference in our journey here on earth". The more we give the more we get. I truly believe that this is God's Law."

God loves a cheerful giver".

HOW TO BECOME A POWER NETWORKER:

- » Meet as many new people as you can every day.
- » Build your network to a minimum of 500 contacts.
- » Promote yourself by introducing yourself or your company.
- » Be a people person—be friendly and polite.
- » Treat others the way you would like to be treated.
- » Love everyone; forgive your enemies.
- » Have a business card and hand it out at every opportunity.

TIPS FOR OVERDOERS

(Adapted from *Overdoing It: How to Slow Down and Take Care of Yourself* by Dr. Bryan Robinson, Health Communications, 1992.)

1. **SLOW DOWN.** Give yourself extra time to get to appointments. Make a conscious effort to walk, eat, and talk slowly.
2. **SAY NO.** When you are overloaded, don't take on new projects.
3. **TAKE CARE OF YOURSELF.** Eat properly, exercise regularly, and get enough sleep.
4. **HURRY UP AND BE PATIENT.** The sooner you become patient, the sooner you will be able to enjoy life to the fullest. Patience creates confidence and encourages rational decision making.
5. **WORK SMARTER.** Work toward your goals but don't let your schedule run your life. Let others share the load.
6. **TAKE TIME FOR RELATIONSHIPS.** Take time to enjoy friends and share intimate and quality time with your family.

FIND RELAXATION THAT WORKS FOR YOU. Whether it is a power nap, a warm bath, or an energizing workout, if it helps you relax, then it is worth the time.

Chapter 10
BECOME SUCCESSFUL: TAKE CARE OF YOURSELF SO YOU CAN TAKE CARE OF OTHERS

The greatest thing a person can do in this world is to make the most possible out of stuff that has been given…
This is success and there is no other. —Orison Swett Marden

The important thing really is not the deed well done or the medal that you possess, but the dedication and dreams out of which they grow. —Bob Benson

What counts is not the number of hours you put in, but how much you put into the hours.

If I take care of my character, my reputation will take care of itself. —Dwight L. Moody

I have not met anyone in my life who did not want to be successful. Everyone wants to be liked, to by wealthy, to be healthy, and to be a SOMEONE. However, life seems to throw us a curve ball every once in a while. These could be minor or major interruptions in our lives. How many times do we plan something and believe that it is what we need to do to create that success that we so crave, and then the rug gets pulled out from under us? How do we handle these roadblocks? Who is putting up these barriers to our success? Who is throwing us off track or what is barring us from getting what we want? Well, there are many things that cause these interruptions. The main barriers to achievement usually are the problem with our thinking. If we have doubts about the outcome, then success will not come. Too many of us are worry warts. We worry about things that have not happened and perhaps never will. I know that, for many years, I would worry about what might happen and would not be able to sleep. Worrying all night, thinking, what if this happens, what will I do? What if something else happens, and then what do I do? Then I would have a virtually sleepless night and look haggard and tired in the morning, and none of these horrible things that I worried about happened. Most of us are worriers, and we blame it on our parents. If your mother was a worrier, then we say that we are too. It took me years to overcome this, and now I sleep well every night. If it hasn't happened, then I don't worry about it. My recent health issues with my lungs took several months to diagnose, and even now the specialists are still not certain what could have caused the lung inflammation and are not 100% sure if the medications that I am taking will cure me. A few people have asked me if I am worried that it could be lung cancer. I am not worried and will not become stressed out over what is not true. If and when the doctors tell me that it is cancer, then, and only then, will I have some concerns. If they determine that it is lung cancer, then I will go and start treatment to beat it and get cured. I have already beaten cancer three times and will beat a fourth one if needed.

Lack of self-confidence is the issue—doubt in our abilities, thinking we are not smart enough, not good enough, don't know if we can do it. If we are prone to negative thinking, about our abilities, and ourselves, then doubt creeps in and we fail to carry on and do what is required to become successful. Calgary's successful entrepreneur. Brett Wilson calls it graduating from Cancer, not surviving.

If you worry about something, does it help? Think about it, if worrying helps then double up on your worrying. Worry causes stress, and stress creates many side effects. Stress compromises our immune systems and we get sick. Then we worry more and just get sicker and sicker. Worry can bring on colds, flu, strokes, heart attacks, cancer, and other debilitating diseases. It took me many years, at bedtime, to be able to just block out any thought of what might happen today and what might happen tomorrow. I am now able to turn my thoughts and mind to either just plain blank or if my mind doesn't want to co-operate, then I start to think of things that are pleasant, perhaps visualizing a peaceful lake, a beach in Australia or Hawaii, or a beautiful lake in Manitoba or the wilds of northern Canada. Just think of something that is pleasant, peaceful, and beautiful. Those problems that we will face probably will not happen, and even if we do have to face challenges tomorrow, sleep well; those challenges will wait and still be there when we wake up well rested and refreshed next morning.

Worry, stress, anger are all killers of our bodies and of our minds. How can we, then, overcome these bad habits that so many of us have formed and hang on to? First, decide that these problems, whether real or imagined, will pass or not materialize. Nothing lasts forever. In the Bible it states, "This too shall pass."

Self-confidence and self-esteem are vital to our ability to succeed in life. If you are a success in life then you will be a success in your career.

Let's look at the difference between self-confidence and self-esteem.

What's worth more to you: something that you've earned or something that some random person gave to you? Exactly, and that is the difference between self-confidence and self-esteem. Self-esteem is a misnomer. Self-esteem is what we develop if we have people telling us you're wonderful, smart, good looking, etc. And that's not a bad thing, but it's a poor substitute for real self-confidence. The big difference is that it takes a lot less to destroy self-esteem than it does self-confidence.

Self-confidence is what we develop through improving ourselves and overcoming obstacles. If you have confidence in yourself, you know you're smart, talented, or whatever because you have proven it to yourself.

For example, you may have always known that you are smart and good at science. People told you this was the case, and it was obvious, but it was never a real challenge. You graduated from a good university with good marks. No big deal. Then you got into web design. Some aspects of it were easy, but the design part—not so much. But you worked at it and figured out ways to work around your weaknesses. You've become a damn good web designer through hard work and therefore you are confident in your abilities and it carries over into other aspects of your life.

Another example is becoming a good dancer. You have very little natural ability and get frustrated when you meet people who are naturally good dancers. You practice and become good in spite of your lack of ability and receive some amazing compliments on a regular basis. This helps your self-esteem (as they are external compliments) but they also reinforce your self-confidence. If someone says you are a bad dancer, you're secure enough to either

1. Look at how good they are and possibly agree that, while you're not in their league, you are a good dancer overall, or

2. Realize that they don't know what they are talking about.

Becoming a success hinges on what you do with your life, how hard you work at it, how much time and effort you put into the task at hand. How much do you need to learn to become proficient and even an expert at what your career calls for? How good do you want to be? In my case, I wanted to be good public speaker, but I was absolutely terrified of standing in front of an audience and making a speech. For a long time, I struggled and made a lot of presentations, but I needed to have everything written out for me or I was afraid that I would forget what I was speaking about and get tongue-tied. So what did I do? I took courses. Training initially helped, but I was still not having the confidence that I desired. I joined Toastmasters and I took as many opportunities to be a master of ceremonies as were offered. Today, I have given presentations to as few as three and as many as 600 people. Am I nervous? Only slightly. I now have the self-confidence that I need and wanted for so long? What did I have to do to overcome my fears, and how long did it take? Many years, but it was worth it. If you want something, go after it, and in almost all cases, many of us just give up. Never give up; do what you fear the most. Otherwise, we will be living with that fear all our lives. Jump in, get started; getting started is halfway there.

In the late 1950s, I was travelling in the Prairies, merchandizing Sunkist Citrus, calling on wholesale distributors and on retail stores. Often, when out on the territory, I would be away for two or even three weeks, not coming home on the weekends. During the week, I called on the major customers, and on Saturdays, I would call on the small mom-and-pop stores. The merchandizing division kept track of how many calls we made, what types of displays were set up, how many pieces of display materials were used and so on. The average number of calls made by over 75 merchandisers in North America were about 45 per week. As I was staying over the weekend at some city, and the big retail outlets did not want anyone working in the stores on a Saturday, and rather than hang around my hotel room all day, I would call on the small stores, and some days I would make about 20 extra contacts and I promoted the Sunkist name, not only in the large supermarkets but also in the smaller outlets. This extra effort brought my calls per week up to about 65. This made my record better than most of the other merchandizing staff, which caught the attention of management. I was quickly recognized for this extra effort and was rapidly promoted. In three years with the company, I was made supervisor of the Canadian Division and transferred to the head office for the country in Toronto.

Just by doing all that was required of me and a little bit more, gave me additional recognition, promotion, and increased pay. Also, I always displayed good manners and treated everyone with respect. It takes very little extra effort to be extraordinary.

WHAT MUST WE DO TO BE SUCCESSFUL?

» Have a dream.
» Dream BIG.
» Learn all you can about what you want to become.
» Don't talk yourself out of what you want from your life.
» Work hard at what you do.
» Do all that is required and then just a little bit more.
» If you are not fully confident, act like you are: fake it until you make it.
» Never give up.
» Never go into anything half-heartedly or you'll get half-hearted results.

YOU WILL NEVER BE SORRY

For thinking before acting.

For hearing before judging.

For forgiving your enemies.

For helping a fallen brother.

For being honest in business.

For standing by your principles.

For stopping your ears to gossip.

For bridling a slanderous tongue.

For harbouring only pure thoughts.

For sympathizing with the afflicted.

For being courteous to all.

TO BE A SUCCESS

Strategy #1. Be the best at what you do; develop EXCELLENCE in all you do.

Strategy #2. Don't focus on perfection, focus on PROGRESS.

Strategy #3. Envision your SUCCESS; plan your work to succeed.

Strategy #4. Develop a WINNING ATTITUDE and infect others.

Strategy #5. Invest in your EDUCATION: focus on learning more and improving your skills.

Strategy #6. Believe in a greater Power; God is the ultimate power.

Chapter 11
KEEP UP WITH TECHNOLOGY

Listen more— talk less.

Stay occupied, be busy, learn something new every day.

You only have one life to live; enjoy this one-and-only journey.

*Happiness lies in the joy of achievement
and the thrill of creative effort.*   —Franklin Roosevelt

Don't reinvent the wheel, just keep it rolling.

Look for the obvious. Break the rules but for the right reasons.

Look for better ways to do things; practice divergent thinking.

Give solutions not problems.

*It isn't what you know but what
you are willing to learn.*   —Clifford Dean Schimmels

It doesn't matter how old we are: some of us will embrace the
changes happening in our lives, while others tell you that they are

too old for that stuff. Well, get with it; you will be left behind if you don't get on the bandwagon. Cell phones are here to stay, and they will change rapidly in the immediate future; in fact, they are changing right now. Computers are getting smaller, with greater capacity and ability to do more month by month. If you don't have a computer or a cell phone, you are in the dark. The newspaper is going the way of the dinosaur. How many of the major daily papers have already disappeared, and how many more will be gone soon? Communication has changed; we are now able to connect with others anywhere in the world in an instant. News reports of events anywhere in this big wide world of ours are available to us through a variety of communications devices and services. If you are not up on the latest technology, then you are missing out in life.

The problem today is that most people are not using this technology for the best and most useful purposes, for what they are meant to be. The cell phone, for example, is certainly handy and great for connecting with others. However, it is now abused, and it is a distraction when improperly used; for example, while driving. The number one cause of car crashes in the United States today is texting. It is equally as serious here in Canada. This is becoming a national crisis; distracted driving is not only dangerous but also can be fatal.

Modern technology, properly used, is a boon to all humanity. It has improved our lives dramatically, and at the same time is creating some problems. The issues of distraction, etc., can be easily corrected. For example, stop using the phone while driving.

Keep yourself and others safe. Become a computer geek; the information age is on the computer and it is instant. Look up anything on your computer and the information is there right at your fingertips. Use technology to become more knowledgeable.

I was for a long time one of those people who fought the move to technology. I was afraid of computers and refused to get a cell phone. But as time went on, I found that I was out of touch with the day. At the time that I was a realtor, I had a pager, but not a cell phone, and I soon found that I was not too efficient. Several clients said a few things that prompted me to get one. Then, when I formed my own food brokerage, I required a computer to operate the office with greater efficiency. I even took a course; however, I am still not as good as I could be, but somehow, I am now getting better. I have gone through two laptops, and basically I use a computer every day in my work, and at home too.

HOW DO WE KEEP UP WITH TECHNOLOGY?

» Believe in the future.
» Have a purpose larger than yourself.
» Exceed beyond your wildest dreams.
» Learn something new at every opportunity.
» Keep up with the times.
» Learn one new word every day.
» Never give up.

TEN RULES FOR A SUCCESSFUL AND LONG LIFE

1. Less meat, more vegetables.
2. Less sugar, more fruit.
3. Less worry, more sleep.
4. Less greed, more charity.
5. Less riding, more walking.
6. Less salt, more vinegar.
7. Less food, more chewing.
8. Less griping, more laughing.
9. Less clothing, more bathing.
10. Less talk, more, action.

Chapter 12
STAY YOUNG
ALL YOUR LIFE

If you live to the age of 70, you will have lived 25,550 days.

Joyfulness keeps the heart and face young.
A good laugh makes us better friends with
ourselves and everybody around us. —Orison Swett Marden

Successful people replace the words "wish," "should," and "try" with
"I WILL."

Happiness is not a destination, it is a journey.

Contribute more than complain.

Let every experience be your teacher.

Be present in every moment.

It seems so simple appreciating life for what it is—pleasure and pain,
joy and sorrow.

For the moment, for today at least,
I have learned to be content. —Gloria Gaither

Use the power of the mind. There are so many things we just don't know. Use the power of the Universe or the power of God. Albert Einstein was so revered by us that when he died we preserved his brain for study. But they found that the brain is just an internal organ, nothing more; we are greater than the sum of our parts and that greatness is found in our spiritual being. We are not human beings having a spiritual experience; we are spiritual beings having a human experience.

I want to share an event that occurred to me in 1992. In April of that year, my wife and I were living in Edmonton and took a trip to Rossburn, Manitoba, to visit her mother and father. On the way there, we stopped in a nearby flower shop and purchased some flowers for her. She was thrilled to see us and also happy to get the flowers.

The following morning, I arose early and drove, by myself, to my hometown, about 40 miles away, where my mother and father are buried. The morning was fresh and clean; it had rained overnight and the countryside was wet and magnificent on a beautiful spring day. I stopped briefly at the little church near the graves of my parents and offered a Prayer for them and all my uncles, aunts, and grandparents, and other people who I remembered who rested in this peaceful graveyard.

As I walked through the grass and the gravel I noticed so many beautiful silk flowers adorning the head stones. There were all colours and varieties, and I felt my heart sink as I realized I had not brought some silk flowers to place on my parents' headstone. I recalled being in that flower shop the day before, and that I could have easily bought them then, but I hadn't thought of it.

It was now too late to do anything about it except to pray and ask God to remind me somehow to get some white silk roses the next time I came here. My mother loved white roses.

I walked back to my car feeling a bit heavy hearted. I remember looking at the ground and stepping around the puddles from the abundant overnight rain. Even though I avoided the puddles, by the time I reached the car, my shoes were wet.

I opened the car door and as I looked down to avoid another puddle, there, lying on the gravel, was a single silk white rose. I scooped it up and looked around to see who may have dropped it because it was not there when I had stepped out of the car earlier. I was alone in that churchyard. No one had come or gone in the last while or I would have heard or noticed them. I walked back to my mother and father's grave holding the silk rose in awe. Having gently placed the flower on their headstone, I withdrew my hand then noticed the best miracle of all. The silk rose was completely clean and dry, even though I had just picked from the rain-soaked ground.

This is one of those incredible examples of that spiritual part of our lives, which we so often ignore. We get so caught up in the physical that we miss this other part of ourselves, which is so indispensable for complete health and well-being. Some may call it coincidence; I believe it to be synchronicity with God. This was the time when I really connected to God with a pain that He really wanted healed. There are times when our prayers are answered in the most miraculous ways and we are offered a glimpse into the real world of our spiritual side.

There are many signs from God that we miss because we fail to connect with Him. Each and every day, there are indications that God is near. He appears to us in various and numerous ways— through people, nature, birds, butterflies, and other signs that we don't notice because we are so wrapped up in our everyday challenges. My wife gets messages from robins. She believes that God sends the birds at times, and from that she gets some clarity that is needed.

Stop and smell the roses, stop and spend time with your family. Do something for others, and don't expect anything in return. If you give, you will receive more in return, just don't expect it immediately. Be useful!

If we believe that we have energy, then we will have energy. If we tell ourselves that we are so tired, then we will be tired. Tell yourself that you love life; be grateful for what you have; don't dwell on what you don't have.

If we are negative, we attract negativity. Positive thinking and action brings us good things. The best way to stay young is to think young. Live your life without stress. Stress is the biggest aging element. If we worry, we don't sleep well, we compromise the immune system. Lack of sleep and stress causes illnesses and wrinkles. Often stress also causes us to overeat and gain weight, which can cause additional illnesses. When we worry, we don't think straight and make poor decisions. Use the power of the mind and relax.

I used to be a worrier, but I gave it up as it didn't do me any good, didn't solve my problems; in fact, it created more problems and more stress. I now forget and forgive.

In recalling my cancer journey, three times I was stricken and three times I beat it. I totally depended on the medical profession and prayed a lot, bringing God into the healing process. I also shared the news of my health issues with my family and friends; we all need support, sympathy, and prayers. I also believed that I would not die, that with the treatments that the doctors applied, the medications prescribed, and the Prayers by family and friends, I was positive that all would turn out well. So what are the results? I am well, healthy and happy, still able to work at several jobs and to volunteer with numerous organizations. By staying involved, we keep ourselves young. Spreading the news, good or bad—in the case of illness, relieves us of much of the stress, and I believe that it lessens the concerns that would weigh us down if we had to handle it on our own. All humans are wired to help others, and, each time I went through my battles with cancer, I had so many prayers being sent to God for my healing that I am certain that's why I am still here. My diabetes is under control, for several reasons, watching my diet and the support of all those who love me. Plus, I never gave up!!!!!!

Another way to stay young is remain active all your life, take on challenges and keep moving and doing. Keep both the body and brain engaged, exercise the muscles and the brain. Stave off dementia and prevent atrophy.

HOW TO STAY YOUNG ALL YOUR LIFE:

» Get adequate sleep; establish a good sleep schedule.
» Eat properly—healthy foods and drinks.
» Stay fit—exercise on a regular basis—keep moving.
» Even if you are a workaholic, take time off for yourself.
» Have fun—don't take yourself seriously.
» Be a lifelong learner—strive to become smarter.
» Good grooming—always look your best.
» Dress for success, in clothes that are clean and stylish.
» Don't get angry or upset—it causes wrinkles.
» Give more of your time and (or) money away to others.
» Do or say something nice to two people every day.
» Smile and say Thank you and Please all the time.
» Keep that spark in your life alive.

TAKE TIME

Take time to be funny,
Rejoice in the Lord.
Let laughter explode
And have fun with God's word.
For laughter is healing,
Gives strength to the weak.
God loves to see smiles,
They lift up the meek.

Take time to be silly.
Too many are somber,
Grabbing to control.
Let go and let God's love
Wash over our soul.

For humour is holy.
It sanctifies life.
Replenishes hope,
Undercuts sorrow and
Deflates haughty pride.
So smile and hang on,
Rejoice in life's ride.

—Author Unknown

HOW TO STAY YOUNG

» Throw out all nonessential numbers. This includes age, weight, and height. Let the doctors worry about them. That's why you pay them.

» Keep only cheerful friends. The grouches pull you down.

» Keep learning. Learn more about computers, crafts, gardening, whatever.

» Never let the brain idle. "An idle mind is the devil's workshop." And the devil's name is Alzheimer's.

» Enjoys simple things

» Laugh often, long, and loud. Laugh until you gasp for breath.

» The tears happen. Endure, grieve, and move on. The only person who is with us our entire life is ourselves. Be ALIVE while you are alive.

» Surround yourself with what you love, whether it's family, pets, keepsakes, music, plants, hobbies, whatever. Your home is your refuge.

» Cherish your health. If it is good, preserve it. If it is unstable, improve it. If it is beyond what you can improve, get help.

» Don't take guilt trips. Take a trip to the mall, next province, or a foreign country, but NOT to where the guilt is.

» Tell the people you love that you love them, at every opportunity.

» Don't sweat the petty things, and don't pet the sweaty things.

Tom's Story

This could easily be called, *The Rest of the Story* or *Now You Know* or *Getting To Know You* or *Manitoba Man*. I want to share with you the journey, the challenges, and the successes of one of our choir members, over the past 12 years.

Tom Shindruk is a three-time cancer survivor. 1) In July of 1999, he had a two-and-half-pound tumour removed from his intestine. 2) In 2001, he was diagnosed with prostate cancer and treated with chemo. 3) In 2004, he was again diagnosed with prostate cancer and this time received 38 radiation treatments.

As Tom journeyed with his cancer diagnosis, he started to volunteer with the Canadian Cancer Society and in 2000 helped launch a fund raiser, Relay For Life, as Recruitment Chair. He remained in that position for seven years and was Honorary Chair for three years. The Relay for Life initiative has raised over $20 million since it started in Calgary in 2000. Many of us remember our involvement in this relay . . . Cold, wet, tiring, very emotional, and at the same time, very gratifying.

Since 2000, Tom has also served with CanSurmount, which helps cancer survivors get through their cancer journey, as well as with Cancer Connection, speaking to various groups to create awareness of the importance of early detection and fund raising.

For the past seven years, Tom has been speaking to school kids about "smoking cessation"—encouraging teens to either quit smoking or not to start.

For his dedicated effort, in 2004, Tom received a Certificate of Appreciation from the Canadian Cancer Society. In 2006, he received the Distinguished Service Award. In 2010, he received the Dr. Peter Geggy Award for Distinguished Community Engagement.

Tom has been the media spokesperson for the Canadian Cancer Society since 2004 doing television, radio, and newspaper interviews and continues to volunteer with the Society in various capacities.

In February of 2013, Tom received the Queen Elizabeth Diamond Jubilee Award for his continued dedication to the cancer cause from the Government of Canada. This same year, he was also given the Medal of Courage by the Canadian Cancer Society.

A note that has to be added here is that 25 years ago, 25% of the people who were diagnosed with cancer survived. Today, there is a 75% survival rate. Much of this success is because of the work of the Canadian Cancer Society, their volunteers, and leaders such as Tom.

In 2011, Tom was suddenly stricken with internal hemorrhaging, largely owing to all the invasive treatments for this cancers. He received nine units of blood in three days and spent a week at the Foothills Hospital.

He received no treatment other than the blood. It is Tom's belief that he was healed with the gift of blood and a miracle from God. In gratitude, he has volunteered with the CBS for the last two years and is presently serving as a member of the Alberta Regional Liaison Committee of the CBS.

Challenges never stop, and recently Tom has been diagnosed with diabetes, but as you know, nothing slows Tom down!

If you want something done, ask a busy person. Tom is currently the Board Chair of Developmental Disabilities Resource Foundation and the Developmental Disabilities Resource Centre in Calgary. He has served on this board for six years. The board consists of 7 members, while the Centre has a staff of 225 who assist individuals who are developmentally challenged.

For the past three years, Tom is also a facilitator with Families Matter and the Be a Great Dad program, which helps divorced and separated dads to reconnect with their children.

Oh, did you know that Tom also works part time? Yep! He provides classroom instruction in "Safe Driving" to the Oil and Gas Industry. He loves this part of his life because he gets to meet people from many parts of the world.

I have to add that Tom also occupies a seat in the Bass section of our St. Stephen's choir loft and is also a K of C. member. And he is closer to 80 than 75 years young. To sum it up—what an amazing journey! And this only covers the last 12 years.

—Compiled by Pat Ochitwa for St. Stephens choir

Additional
EXTRAORDINARY
MESSAGES

Believe in yourself.

You are your own greatest asset—there is nothing you cannot do.

No one can keep you from dreaming your dreams, and only you can prevent them from coming true.

Your achievements are not determined by your ability alone, but by the desire you possess to reach them.

There are no worlds outside those you create for yourself, and the only boundaries are those you establish and choose to live within.

Never be afraid to defend your decisions, regardless. No one can possibly know what is best for you other than yourself.

—Terry Everton

Count your garden by the flowers,
Never by the leaves that fall.
Count your days by golden hours,
Don't remember clouds at all.
Count your nights by stars, not shadows,
Count your life with smiles, not tears.
And your joy on every birthday,
Count your age by friends, not years.

—Italian Philosophy

I am going to be happy today!
Though the skies are cloudy and gray,
No matter what comes my way—
I'm going to be happy today!   —Ella Wheeler Wilcox

"Success Is Never Certain and Failure Is Never Final"

❖

A bell is no bell, till you ring it,
A song is no song, till you sing it,
And love in your heart
Wasn't put there to stay—
Love isn't love
Until you give it away.
                    —Oscar Hammerstein wrote in *The Sound of Music*

❖

Love is a verb as well as a noun
Love means a smile and never a frown
To love is to do and not just to feel
For unless you express it, love is not real.   —Odell McConnell

❖

Love sees not what we are,
but what we may become.

❖

TOM SHINDRUK

Doubt blinds you to possibilities!
But faith opens your eyes to new opportunities!

—Robert H. Schuller

HOW TO DELIVER A POSITIVE ATTITUDE

FOCUS ON STRENGTHS – Negative reinforcement is just as powerful as positive reinforcement.

POSITIVE SELF-TALK – Eliminate awful-ising, should-ising, over general-ising and catastroph-isisng. Keep self-talk positive, empowering and supporting.

SMILE – This is a simple "random act of kindness" that makes others (and you) feel good. Others want to hang around someone who smiles.

SHOW A PERSONAL INTEREST IN OTHERS – Ask questions about others in their family, their workplace and their community.

FACILITATE DISCUSSION – About "what is going well" or "best parts" of what is going on in your family, community or work life.

LISTEN – Set aside your own agenda, ego and emotions, and truly listen to understand the other person's perspective. Listen with "empathy" rather than "sympathy."

ATTITUDE OF GRATITUDE – Praise partial successes and effort (yours and others). Big successes usually have small beginnings.

DEMONSTRATE YOUR AFFECTION –
Appropriately show others that you CARE about
them and their lives.

LIVE WITH INTEGRITY – Do what you say and
say what you do. Make and keep clear, conscious
agreement with self and others.

BE ACCOUNTABLE – Be aware that you are the
"captain of your ship." Everything that has happened, or will happen, to you has been a result of
your choices at some level of circumstances.

MAKE WISE CHOICES – Understand that a
positive attitude is a choice that you can make at
any time and in any circumstance.

—Dan Ohler from *Thinkin' Outside the Barn! And
Steppin' Into Fresh B.S.*

Don't kill the dream—execute it!

You don't have to be great to start,
but you have to start to be great.
                                        —Joe Sabah

RULES TO LOOK AND STAY YOUNG

1. Shape up
2. Get enough sleep
3. Proper diet
4. Exercise program
5. Avoid poisons
6. Give it your best effort
7. THINK "YOUNG"

IT'S NOT EASY . . .

To apologize,
To begin over,
To be unselfish,
To take advice,
To admit error,
To face a sneer,
To be charitable,
To keep trying,
To be considerate,
To avoid mistakes,
To endure success,
To profit by mistakes,
To forgive and forget,
To keep out of a rut,
To make the best of little,
To subdue and unruly temper,
To shoulder a deserved blame,
To recognize the silver lining—
BUT IT ALWAYS PAYS

PROFESSIONALISM

Professionalism has nothing to do with position, status or salary.
Professionalism is an attitude not education—Performance
not Promises.
Being a professional means being serious about your work and
dedicated to it.
Professional is—The Pursuit of Excellence   —Catherine Ford

QUOTATIONS TO PONDER

Commitment with accountability closes
the gap between intention and results.   —Sandra Gallagher

The greatest day in your life and mine is when we take total
responsibility for our attitudes. That's the day we truly grow up.
                                              —John C. Maxwell

We must develop a network of leaders, drawn from all segments,
who accept some measure of responsibility for the community's shared
concerns. I call them networks of responsibility, leaders of disparate or
conflicting interests who undertake to act collaboratively on behalf of
the shared concerns of the community and the nation.
                                              —John W. Gardner

One's philosophy is not best expressed in words; it is expressed in the
choices one makes. In the long run, we shape our lives and we shape
ourselves. The process never ends until we die. And, the choices we
make are ultimately our own responsibility.   —Eleanor Roosevelt

POPE FRANCIS' 10 TIPS FOR A HAPPIER LIFE

1. "Live and let live." Everyone should be guided by this principle, he said, which has a similar expression in Rome with the saying, "Move forward and let others do the same."

2. "Be giving of yourself to others." People need to be open and generous toward others, he said, because "if you withdraw into yourself, you run the risk of becoming egocentric. And stagnant water becomes putrid."

3. "Proceed calmly" in life. The pope, who used to teach high school literature, used an image from an Argentine novel by Ricardo Guiraldes, in which the protagonist—gaucho Don Segundo Sombra—looks back on how he lived his life.

4. A healthy sense of leisure. The Pope said "consumerism has brought us anxiety," and told parents to set aside time to play with their children and turn off the TV when they sit down to eat.

5. Sundays should be holidays. Workers should have Sundays off because "Sunday is for family," he said.

6. Find innovative ways to create dignified jobs for young people. "We need to be creative with young people. If they have no opportunities they will get into drugs" and be more vulnerable to suicide, he said.

7. Respect and take care of nature. Environmental degradation "is one of the biggest challenges we have," he said. "I think a question that we're not asking ourselves is: 'Isn't humanity committing suicide with this indiscriminate and tyrannical use of nature?'"

8. Stop being negative. "Needing to talk badly about others indicates low self-esteem. That means, 'I feel so low that instead of picking myself up I have to cut others down,'"

the Pope said. "Letting go of negative things quickly is healthy."

9. Don't proselytize; respect others' beliefs. "We can inspire others through witness so that one grows together in communicating. But the worst thing of all is religious proselytism, which paralyses: 'I am talking with you in order to persuade you,' No. Each person dialogues, starting with his and her own identity. The church grows by attraction, not proselytizing," the Pope said.

10. Work for peace. "We are living in a time of many wars," he said, and "the call for peace must be shouted. Peace sometimes gives the impression of being quiet, but it is never quiet, peace is always proactive" and dynamic.

It's Not What You Gather, But What You Scatter That Tells What Kind of Life You Have Lived.

CPSIA information can be obtained
at www.ICGtesting.com
Printed in the USA
BVHW082029201121
622062BV00003B/9